Open thou mine eyes,
that I may behold
wondrous things
out of thy law.

Psalm 119:18

Date

Meeting Notes

Circle what meeting it is

Memorial   Lecture

Bible Class   CYC

Study Day   Other

Presider

Uncle_____

Speaker

Uncle_____

Title of the talk or main theme

Bible reading/s

Bible passages referred to in the talk

Hymns

Notes from the talk

_____

_____

_____

_____

_____

_____

_____

_____

_____

_____

_____

_____

_____

Drawing or key verse

Date

Meeting Notes

Circle what meeting it is

Memorial	Lecture
Bible Class	CYC
Study Day	Other

Presider

Uncle_____

Speaker

Uncle_____

Title of the talk or main theme

Bible reading/s

Bible passages referred to in the talk

Hymns

Notes from the talk

_____
_____
_____
_____
_____
_____
_____
_____
_____
_____
_____
_____
_____
_____

Drawing or key verse

Date

Meeting Notes

Circle what meeting it is

Memorial	Lecture
Bible Class	CYC
Study Day	Other

Presider

Uncle_____

Speaker

Uncle_____

Title of the talk or main theme

Bible reading/s

Bible passages referred to in the talk

Hymns

Notes from the talk

Drawing or key verse

Date

Meeting Notes

Circle what meeting it is

Memorial	Lecture
Bible Class	CYC
Study Day	Other

Presider

Uncle_____

Speaker

Uncle_____

Title of the talk or main theme

Bible reading/s

Bible passages referred to in the talk

Hymns

Notes from the talk

_____

_____

_____

_____

_____

_____

_____

_____

_____

_____

_____

_____

_____

_____

_____

_____

_____

Drawing or key verse

Date

Meeting Notes

Circle what meeting it is

Memorial   Lecture

Bible Class   CYC

Study Day   Other

Presider

Uncle_____

Speaker

Uncle_____

Title of the talk or main theme

Bible reading/s

Bible passages referred to in the talk

Hymns

Notes from the talk

_____

_____

_____

_____

_____

_____

_____

_____

_____

_____

_____

_____

_____

Drawing or key verse

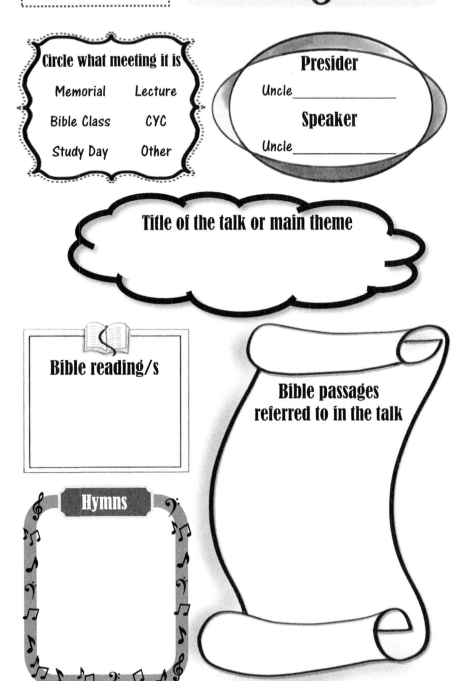

Date

Meeting Notes

Circle what meeting it is

Memorial   Lecture

Bible Class   CYC

Study Day   Other

Presider

Uncle_____

Speaker

Uncle_____

Title of the talk or main theme

Bible reading/s

Bible passages referred to in the talk

Hymns

Notes from the talk

_____

_____

_____

_____

_____

_____

_____

_____

_____

_____

_____

_____

_____

_____

Drawing or key verse

Date

Meeting Notes

Circle what meeting it is

Memorial	Lecture
Bible Class	CYC
Study Day	Other

Presider

Uncle_____

Speaker

Uncle_____

 **Title of the talk or main theme**

Bible reading/s

Bible passages referred to in the talk

Hymns

Notes from the talk

Drawing or key verse

Date

Meeting Notes

Circle what meeting it is

Memorial | Lecture

Bible Class | CYC

Study Day | Other

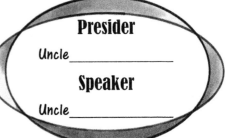

Presider

Uncle_____

Speaker

Uncle_____

Title of the talk or main theme

Bible reading/s

Bible passages referred to in the talk

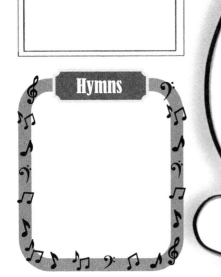

Hymns

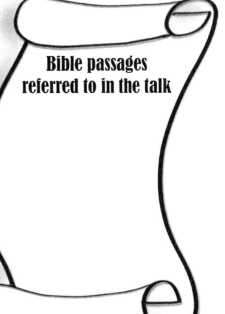

Notes from the talk

_____
_____
_____
_____
_____
_____
_____
_____
_____
_____
_____
_____
_____
_____

Drawing or key verse

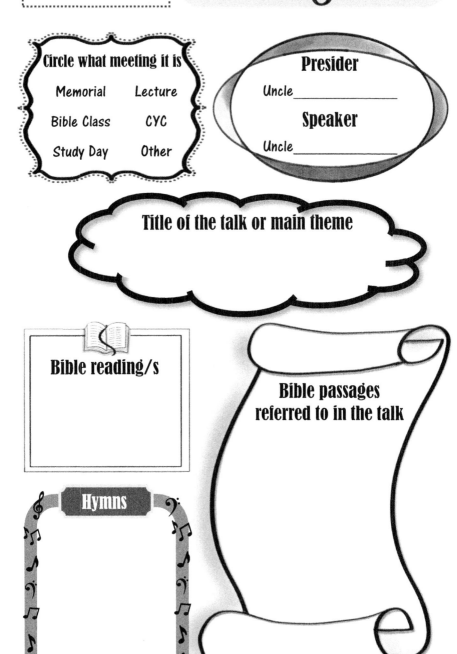

Notes from the talk

_____

_____

_____

_____

_____

_____

_____

_____

_____

_____

_____

_____

Drawing or key verse

_____

_____

_____

_____

_____

_____

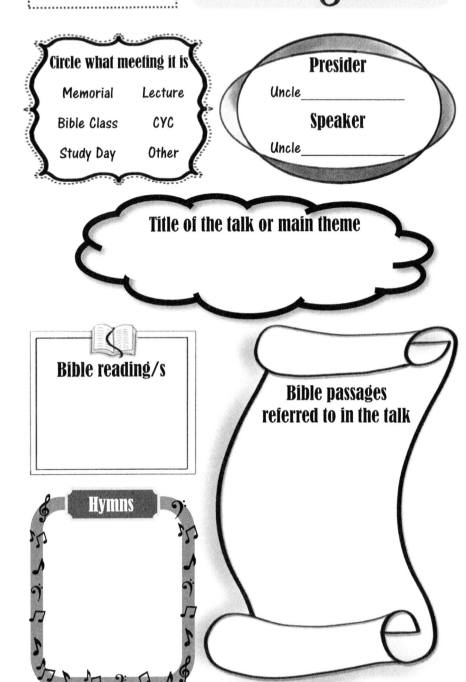

Notes from the talk

_____

_____

_____

_____

_____

_____

_____

_____

_____

_____

_____

_____

_____

_____

Drawing or key verse

_____

_____

_____

_____

Date

Meeting Notes

Circle what meeting it is

Memorial   Lecture

Bible Class   CYC

Study Day   Other

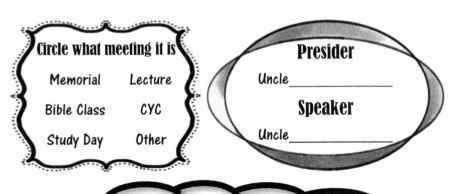

Presider

Uncle_____

Speaker

Uncle_____

Title of the talk or main theme

Bible reading/s

Bible passages referred to in the talk

Hymns

Notes from the talk

Drawing or key verse

Date

Meeting Notes

Circle what meeting it is

Memorial	Lecture
Bible Class	CYC
Study Day	Other

Presider

Uncle_____

Speaker

Uncle_____

Title of the talk or main theme

Bible reading/s

Bible passages referred to in the talk

Hymns

Notes from the talk

Drawing or key verse

Date

Meeting Notes

Circle what meeting it is

Memorial	Lecture
Bible Class	CYC
Study Day	Other

Presider

Uncle_____

Speaker

Uncle_____

Title of the talk or main theme

Bible reading/s

Bible passages referred to in the talk

Hymns

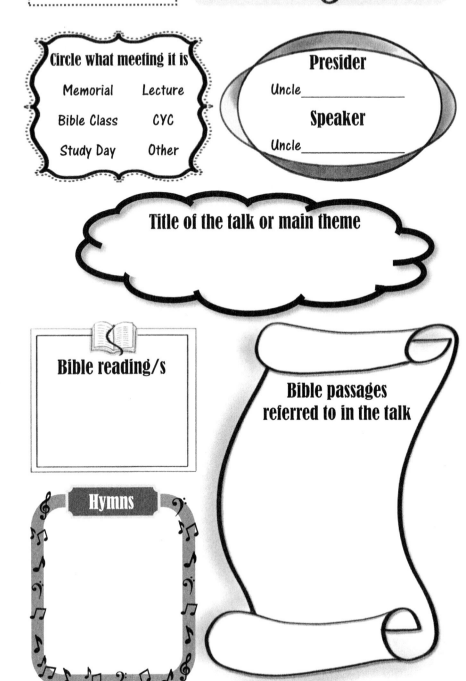

Notes from the talk

_____

_____

_____

_____

_____

_____

_____

_____

_____

_____

_____

_____

_____

Drawing or key verse

_____

_____

_____

Date

Meeting Notes

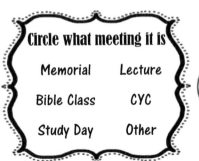

Circle what meeting it is

Memorial	Lecture
Bible Class	CYC
Study Day	Other

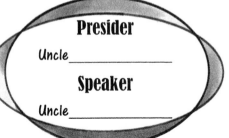

Presider

Uncle_____

Speaker

Uncle_____

Title of the talk or main theme

Bible reading/s

Hymns

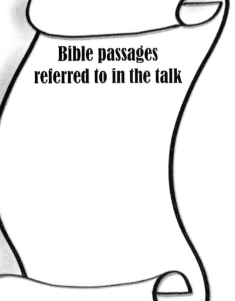

Bible passages referred to in the talk

Notes from the talk

Drawing or key verse

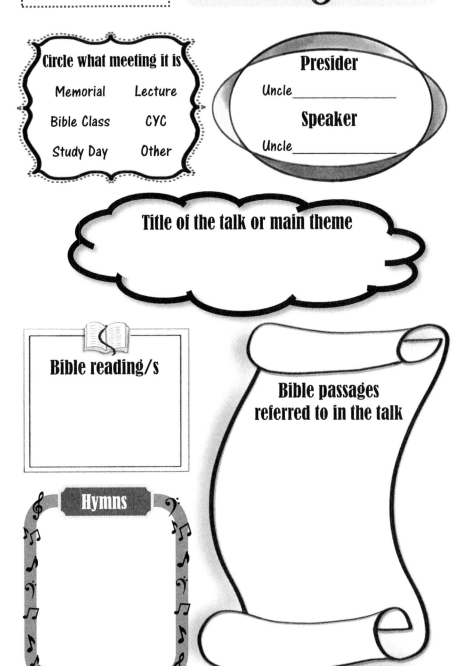

Notes from the talk

_____
_____
_____
_____
_____
_____
_____
_____
_____
_____
_____
_____
_____
_____
_____
_____

Drawing or key verse

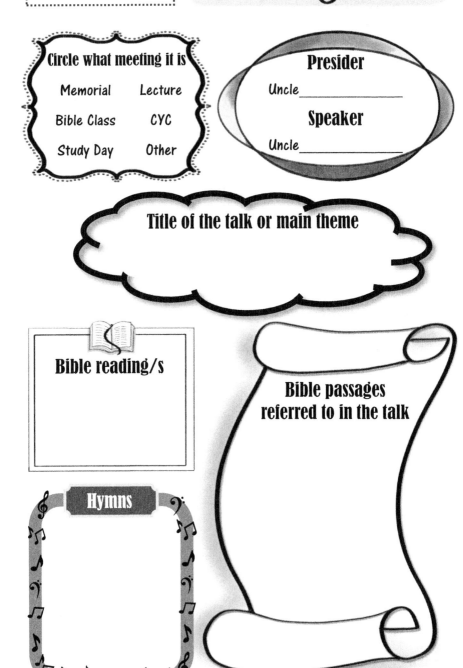

Date

Meeting Notes

Circle what meeting it is

Memorial	Lecture
Bible Class	CYC
Study Day	Other

Presider

Uncle_____

Speaker

Uncle_____

Title of the talk or main theme

Bible reading/s

Bible passages referred to in the talk

Hymns

Notes from the talk

_____

_____

_____

_____

_____

_____

_____

_____

_____

_____

_____

_____

_____

_____

_____

_____

_____

_____

_____

_____

Drawing or key verse

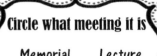

Meeting Notes

Circle what meeting it is

Memorial	Lecture
Bible Class	CYC
Study Day	Other

Presider

Uncle_____

Speaker

Uncle_____

Title of the talk or main theme

Bible reading/s

Bible passages referred to in the talk

Hymns

Notes from the talk

_____
_____
_____
_____
_____
_____
_____
_____
_____
_____
_____
_____
_____
_____

Drawing or key verse

_____
_____
_____
_____

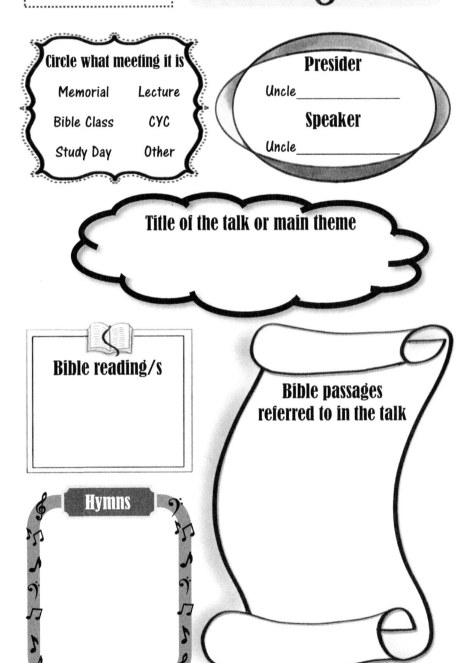

Date

Meeting Notes

Circle what meeting it is

Memorial   Lecture

Bible Class   CYC

Study Day   Other

Presider

Uncle_____

Speaker

Uncle_____

Title of the talk or main theme

Bible reading/s

Bible passages referred to in the talk

Hymns

Notes from the talk

_____
_____
_____
_____
_____
_____
_____
_____
_____
_____
_____
_____
_____
_____
_____
_____
_____
_____
_____

Drawing or key verse

Date

Meeting Notes

Circle what meeting it is

Memorial   Lecture

Bible Class   CYC

Study Day   Other

Presider

Uncle_____

Speaker

Uncle_____

Title of the talk or main theme

Bible reading/s

Bible passages referred to in the talk

Hymns

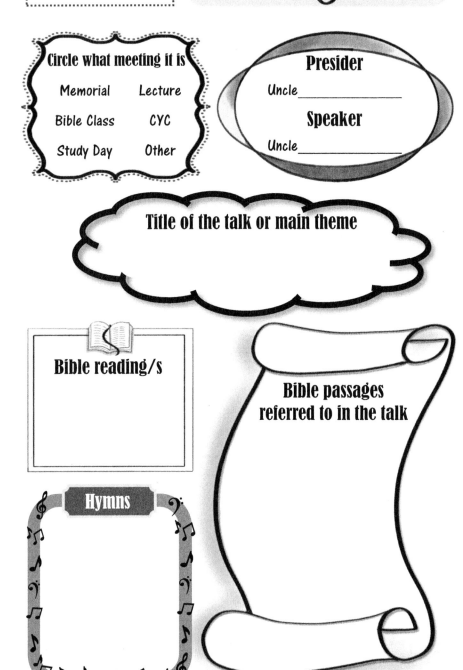

Notes from the talk

Drawing or key verse

Date

Meeting Notes

Circle what meeting it is

Memorial   Lecture

Bible Class   CYC

Study Day   Other

Presider

Uncle_____

Speaker

Uncle_____

Title of the talk or main theme

Bible reading/s

Bible passages referred to in the talk

Hymns

Notes from the talk

Drawing or key verse

Date

Meeting Notes

Circle what meeting it is

Memorial	Lecture
Bible Class	CYC
Study Day	Other

Presider

Uncle_____

Speaker

Uncle_____

Title of the talk or main theme

Bible reading/s

Bible passages referred to in the talk

Hymns

Notes from the talk

_____

_____

_____

_____

_____

_____

_____

_____

_____

_____

_____

_____

_____

_____

_____

_____

Drawing or key verse

_____

_____

_____

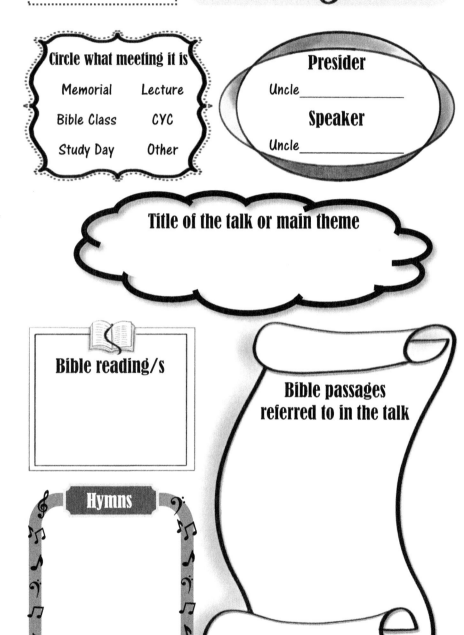

Date

Meeting Notes

Circle what meeting it is

Memorial   Lecture

Bible Class   CYC

Study Day   Other

Presider

Uncle_____

Speaker

Uncle_____

Title of the talk or main theme

Bible reading/s

Bible passages referred to in the talk

Hymns

Notes from the talk

_____

_____

_____

_____

_____

_____

_____

_____

_____

_____

_____

_____

_____

_____

Drawing or key verse

_____

_____

_____

_____

_____

_____

Date

Meeting Notes

Circle what meeting it is

Memorial	Lecture
Bible Class	CYC
Study Day	Other

Presider

Uncle_____

Speaker

Uncle_____

Title of the talk or main theme

Bible reading/s

Bible passages referred to in the talk

Hymns

Notes from the talk

_____
_____
_____
_____
_____
_____
_____
_____
_____
_____
_____
_____
_____
_____
_____

Drawing or key verse

_____
_____
_____
_____

Date

Meeting Notes

Circle what meeting it is

Memorial   Lecture

Bible Class   CYC

Study Day   Other

Presider

Uncle_____

Speaker

Uncle_____

Title of the talk or main theme

Bible reading/s

Bible passages
referred to in the talk

Hymns

Notes from the talk

_____

_____

_____

_____

_____

_____

_____

_____

_____

_____

_____

_____

_____

_____

_____

_____

Drawing or key verse

_____

_____

_____

_____

_____

_____

Date

Meeting Notes

Circle what meeting it is

Memorial   Lecture

Bible Class   CYC

Study Day   Other

Presider

Uncle_____

Speaker

Uncle_____

Title of the talk or main theme

Bible reading/s

Bible passages referred to in the talk

Hymns

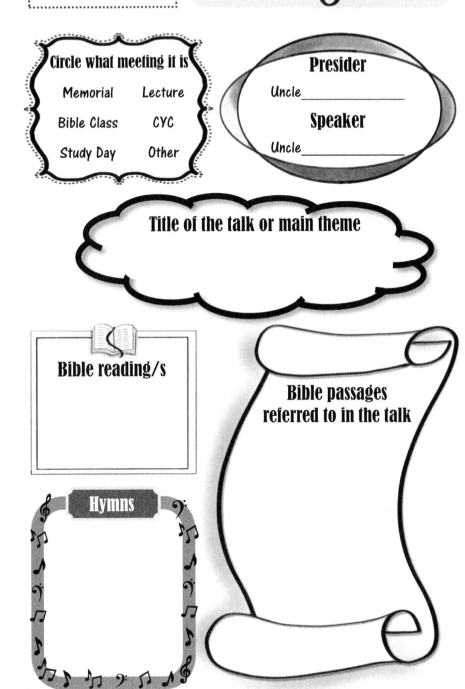

Notes from the talk

_____

_____

_____

_____

_____

_____

_____

_____

_____

_____

_____

_____

_____

_____

_____

_____

Drawing or key verse

_____

_____

_____

_____

Date

Meeting Notes

Circle what meeting it is

Memorial	Lecture
Bible Class	CYC
Study Day	Other

Presider

Uncle_____

Speaker

Uncle_____

Title of the talk or main theme

Bible reading/s

Bible passages referred to in the talk

Hymns

Notes from the talk

_____
_____
_____
_____
_____
_____
_____
_____
_____
_____
_____
_____
_____

Drawing or key verse

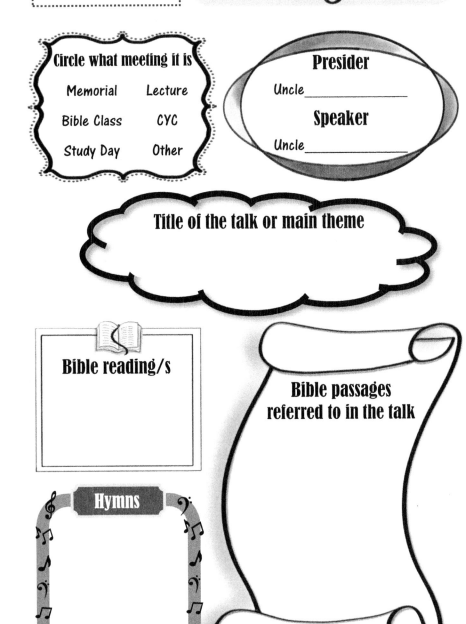

Date

Meeting Notes

Circle what meeting it is

Memorial   Lecture

Bible Class   CYC

Study Day   Other

Presider

Uncle_____

Speaker

Uncle_____

Title of the talk or main theme

Bible reading/s

Bible passages referred to in the talk

Hymns

Notes from the talk

_____

_____

_____

_____

_____

_____

_____

_____

_____

_____

_____

_____

_____

Drawing or key verse

_____

_____

_____

_____

_____

Date

Meeting Notes

Circle what meeting it is

Memorial	Lecture
Bible Class	CYC
Study Day	Other

Presider

Uncle_____

Speaker

Uncle_____

Title of the talk or main theme

Bible reading/s

Bible passages referred to in the talk

Hymns

Notes from the talk

_____

_____

_____

_____

_____

_____

_____

_____

_____

_____

_____

_____

_____

_____

_____

Drawing or key verse

_____

_____

_____

_____

Date

Meeting Notes

Circle what meeting it is

Memorial	Lecture
Bible Class	CYC
Study Day	Other

Presider

Uncle _____

Speaker

Uncle _____

Title of the talk or main theme

Bible reading/s

Bible passages referred to in the talk

Hymns

Notes from the talk

_____
_____
_____
_____
_____
_____
_____
_____
_____
_____
_____

Drawing or key verse

_____
_____
_____
_____

Date

Meeting Notes

Circle what meeting it is

Memorial · Lecture

Bible Class · CYC

Study Day · Other

Presider

Uncle_____

Speaker

Uncle_____

Title of the talk or main theme

Bible reading/s

Bible passages referred to in the talk

Hymns

Notes from the talk

_____
_____
_____
_____
_____
_____
_____
_____
_____
_____
_____
_____
_____
_____

Drawing or key verse

Date

Meeting Notes

Circle what meeting it is

Memorial   Lecture

Bible Class   CYC

Study Day   Other

Presider

Uncle_____

Speaker

Uncle_____

Title of the talk or main theme

Bible reading/s

Bible passages referred to in the talk

Hymns

Notes from the talk

Drawing or key verse

Date

Meeting Notes

Circle what meeting it is

Memorial   Lecture

Bible Class   CYC

Study Day   Other

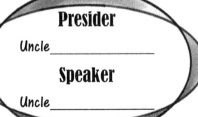

Presider

Uncle_____

Speaker

Uncle_____

Title of the talk or main theme

Bible reading/s

Bible passages referred to in the talk

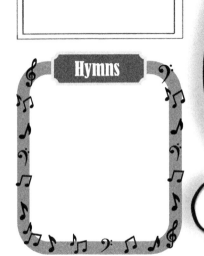 **Hymns**

Notes from the talk

_____

_____

_____

_____

_____

_____

_____

_____

_____

_____

_____

_____

_____

_____

Drawing or key verse

_____

_____

_____

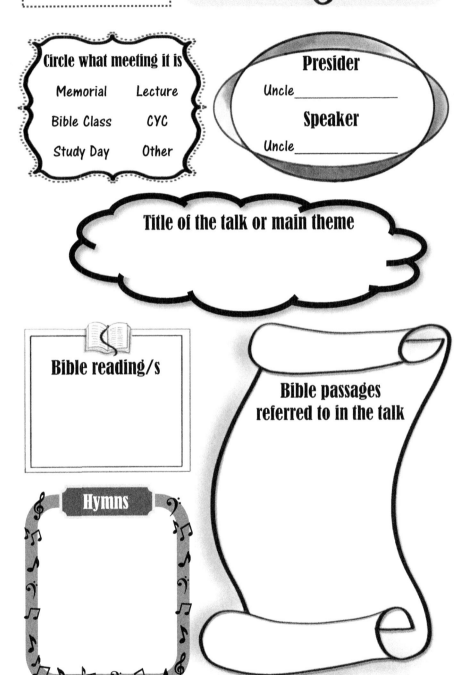

Date

Meeting Notes

Circle what meeting it is

Memorial Lecture

Bible Class CYC

Study Day Other

Presider

Uncle_____

Speaker

Uncle_____

Title of the talk or main theme

Bible reading/s

Bible passages referred to in the talk

Hymns

Notes from the talk

_____

_____

_____

_____

_____

_____

_____

_____

_____

_____

_____

_____

_____

Drawing or key verse

_____

_____

_____

_____

_____

Date

Meeting Notes

Circle what meeting it is

Memorial	Lecture
Bible Class	CYC
Study Day	Other

Presider

Uncle_____

Speaker

Uncle_____

Title of the talk or main theme

Bible reading/s

Bible passages referred to in the talk

Hymns

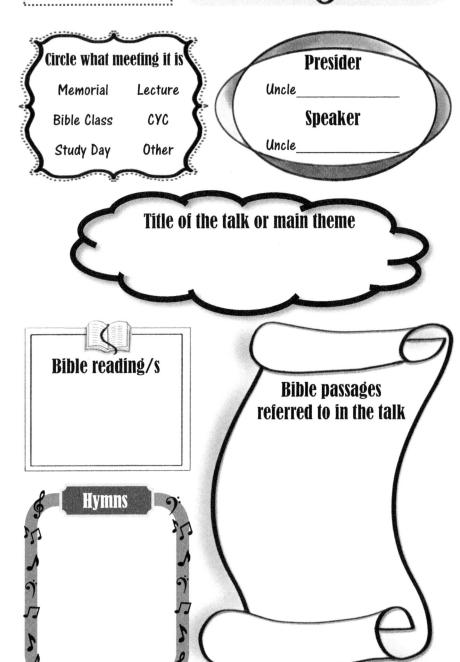

Notes from the talk

_____

_____

_____

_____

_____

_____

_____

_____

_____

_____

_____

_____

_____

_____

_____

_____

_____

_____

_____

Drawing or key verse

Date

Meeting Notes

Circle what meeting it is

Memorial   Lecture

Bible Class   CYC

Study Day   Other

Presider

Uncle _____

Speaker

Uncle _____

Title of the talk or main theme

Bible reading/s

Bible passages referred to in the talk

Hymns

Notes from the talk

_____
_____
_____
_____
_____
_____
_____
_____
_____
_____
_____
_____
_____
_____
_____

Drawing or key verse

Date

Meeting Notes

Circle what meeting it is

Memorial	Lecture
Bible Class	CYC
Study Day	Other

Presider

Uncle_____

Speaker

Uncle_____

Title of the talk or main theme

Bible reading/s

Bible passages referred to in the talk

Hymns

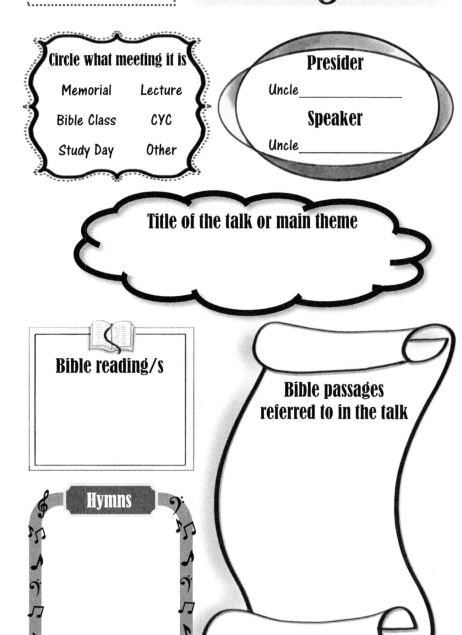

Notes from the talk

_____
_____
_____
_____
_____
_____
_____
_____
_____
_____
_____
_____
_____

Drawing or key verse

Notes from the talk

_____

_____

_____

_____

_____

_____

_____

_____

_____

_____

_____

_____

_____

_____

_____

_____

_____

Drawing or key verse

_____

_____

_____

_____

Meeting Notes

Circle what meeting it is

Memorial	Lecture
Bible Class	CYC
Study Day	Other

Presider

Uncle_____

Speaker

Uncle_____

Title of the talk or main theme

Bible reading/s

Bible passages referred to in the talk

Hymns

Notes from the talk

_____
_____
_____
_____
_____
_____
_____
_____
_____
_____
_____
_____
_____
_____
_____
_____
_____
_____
_____

Drawing or key verse

Circle what meeting it is

Memorial	Lecture
Bible Class	CYC
Study Day	Other

Presider

Uncle_____

Speaker

Uncle_____

Title of the talk or main theme

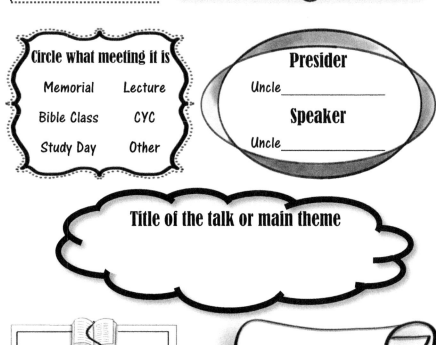
Bible reading/s

Bible passages referred to in the talk

Hymns

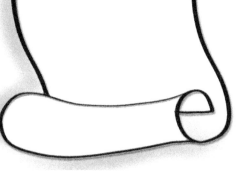

Notes from the talk

_____

_____

_____

_____

_____

_____

_____

_____

_____

_____

_____

_____

Drawing or key verse

_____

_____

_____

_____

Date

Meeting Notes

Circle what meeting it is

Memorial	Lecture
Bible Class	CYC
Study Day	Other

Presider

Uncle_____

Speaker

Uncle_____

Title of the talk or main theme

Bible reading/s

Bible passages referred to in the talk

Hymns

Notes from the talk

_____
_____
_____
_____
_____
_____
_____
_____
_____
_____
_____
_____
_____
_____
_____

Drawing or key verse

Date

Meeting Notes

Circle what meeting it is

Memorial   Lecture

Bible Class   CYC

Study Day   Other

Presider

Uncle_____

Speaker

Uncle_____

Title of the talk or main theme

Bible reading/s

Bible passages referred to in the talk

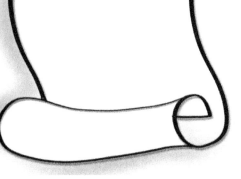

Hymns

Notes from the talk

Drawing or key verse

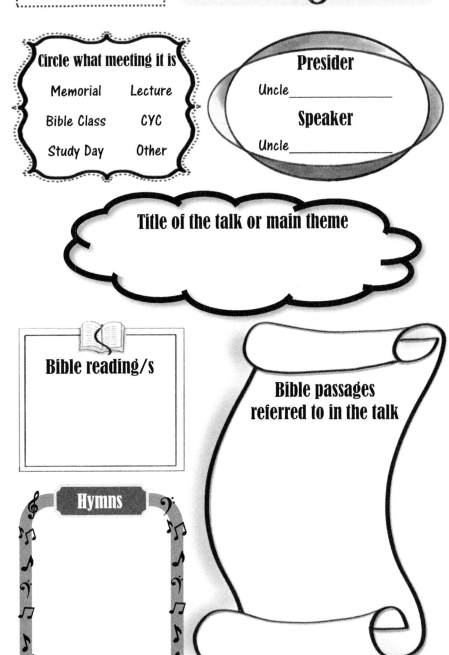

Notes from the talk

_____

_____

_____

_____

_____

_____

_____

_____

_____

_____

_____

_____

_____

Drawing or key verse

_____

_____

_____

_____

Meeting Notes

Circle what meeting it is

Memorial   Lecture

Bible Class   CYC

Study Day   Other

Presider

Uncle_____

Speaker

Uncle_____

Title of the talk or main theme

Bible reading/s

Bible passages referred to in the talk

Hymns

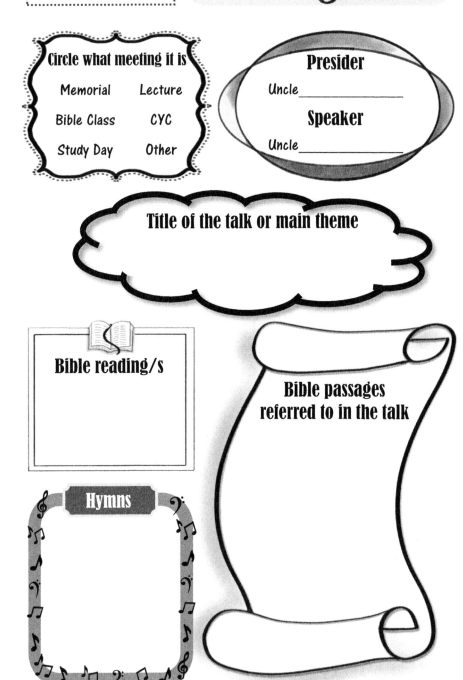

Notes from the talk

_____

_____

_____

_____

_____

_____

_____

_____

_____

_____

_____

_____

_____

_____

_____

_____

Drawing or key verse

_____

_____

_____

_____

Date

Meeting Notes

Circle what meeting it is

Memorial   Lecture

Bible Class   CYC

Study Day   Other

Presider

Uncle_____

Speaker

Uncle_____

Title of the talk or main theme

Bible reading/s

Bible passages referred to in the talk

Hymns

Notes from the talk

Drawing or key verse

Date

Meeting Notes

Circle what meeting it is

Memorial	Lecture
Bible Class	CYC
Study Day	Other

Presider

Uncle_____

Speaker

Uncle_____

Title of the talk or main theme

Bible reading/s

Bible passages referred to in the talk

Hymns

Notes from the talk

_____

_____

_____

_____

_____

_____

_____

_____

_____

_____

_____

_____

_____

_____

_____

Drawing or key verse

Meeting Notes

Circle what meeting it is

Memorial	Lecture
Bible Class	CYC
Study Day	Other

Presider

Uncle_____

Speaker

Uncle_____

Title of the talk or main theme

Bible reading/s

Bible passages referred to in the talk

Hymns

Notes from the talk

_____

_____

_____

_____

_____

_____

_____

_____

_____

_____

_____

_____

_____

_____

_____

Drawing or key verse

_____

_____

_____

_____

Date

Meeting Notes

Circle what meeting it is

Memorial	Lecture
Bible Class	CYC
Study Day	Other

Presider

Uncle_____

Speaker

Uncle_____

Title of the talk or main theme

Bible reading/s

Bible passages referred to in the talk

Hymns

Notes from the talk

Drawing or key verse

Date

Meeting Notes

Circle what meeting it is

Memorial	Lecture
Bible Class	CYC
Study Day	Other

Presider

Uncle_____

Speaker

Uncle_____

Title of the talk or main theme

Bible reading/s

Bible passages referred to in the talk

Hymns

Notes from the talk

_____

_____

_____

_____

_____

_____

_____

_____

_____

_____

_____

_____

_____

Drawing or key verse

_____

_____

_____

_____

Notes from the talk

_____

_____

_____

_____

_____

_____

_____

_____

_____

_____

_____

_____

_____

_____

_____

_____

Drawing or key verse

Date

Meeting Notes

Circle what meeting it is

Memorial	Lecture
Bible Class	CYC
Study Day	Other

Presider

Uncle_____

Speaker

Uncle_____

Title of the talk or main theme

Bible reading/s

Bible passages referred to in the talk

Hymns

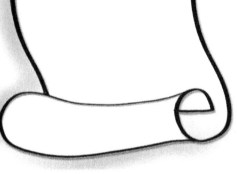

Notes from the talk

_____
_____
_____
_____
_____
_____
_____
_____
_____
_____
_____
_____
_____
_____
_____
_____
_____
_____

Drawing or key verse

Date

Meeting Notes

Circle what meeting it is

Memorial   Lecture

Bible Class   CYC

Study Day   Other

Presider

Uncle_____

Speaker

Uncle_____

Title of the talk or main theme

Bible reading/s

Bible passages referred to in the talk

Hymns

Notes from the talk

_____

_____

_____

_____

_____

_____

_____

_____

_____

_____

_____

_____

_____

_____

_____

_____

_____

Drawing or key verse

_____

_____

_____

_____

_____

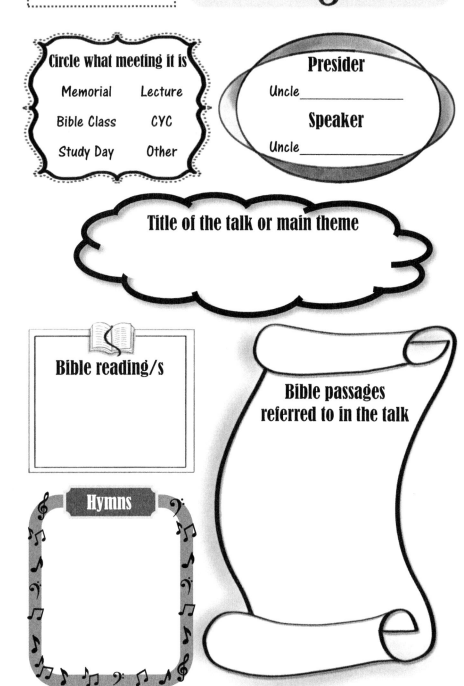

Notes from the talk

_____
_____
_____
_____
_____
_____
_____
_____
_____
_____
_____
_____
_____

Drawing or key verse

_____
_____
_____

Date

Meeting Notes

Circle what meeting it is

Memorial	Lecture
Bible Class	CYC
Study Day	Other

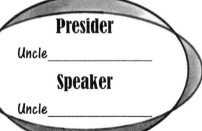

Presider

Uncle_____

Speaker

Uncle_____

Title of the talk or main theme

Bible reading/s

Bible passages referred to in the talk

Hymns

Notes from the talk

_____

_____

_____

_____

_____

_____

_____

_____

_____

_____

_____

_____

_____

_____

_____

Drawing or key verse

Date

Meeting Notes

Circle what meeting it is

Memorial	Lecture
Bible Class	CYC
Study Day	Other

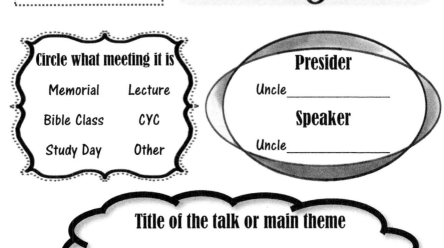

Presider

Uncle_____

Speaker

Uncle_____

Title of the talk or main theme

Bible reading/s

Bible passages referred to in the talk

 **Hymns**

Notes from the talk

_____

_____

_____

_____

_____

_____

_____

_____

_____

_____

_____

_____

_____

Drawing or key verse

_____

_____

_____

_____

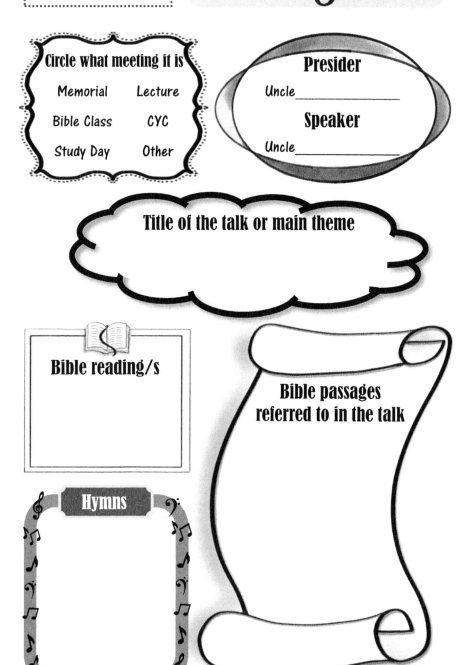

Date

Meeting Notes

Circle what meeting it is

Memorial Lecture

Bible Class CYC

Study Day Other

Presider

Uncle_____

Speaker

Uncle_____

Title of the talk or main theme

Bible reading/s

Bible passages referred to in the talk

Hymns

Notes from the talk

_____

_____

_____

_____

_____

_____

_____

_____

_____

_____

_____

_____

_____

_____

_____

_____

Drawing or key verse

Date

Meeting Notes

Circle what meeting it is

Memorial	Lecture
Bible Class	CYC
Study Day	Other

Presider

Uncle_____

Speaker

Uncle_____

Title of the talk or main theme

Bible reading/s

Bible passages referred to in the talk

Hymns

Notes from the talk

_____

_____

_____

_____

_____

_____

_____

_____

_____

_____

_____

_____

_____

_____

_____

_____

Drawing or key verse

_____

_____

_____

_____

Date

Meeting Notes

Circle what meeting it is

Memorial   Lecture

Bible Class   CYC

Study Day   Other

Presider

Uncle_____

Speaker

Uncle_____

Title of the talk or main theme

Bible reading/s

Bible passages referred to in the talk

Hymns

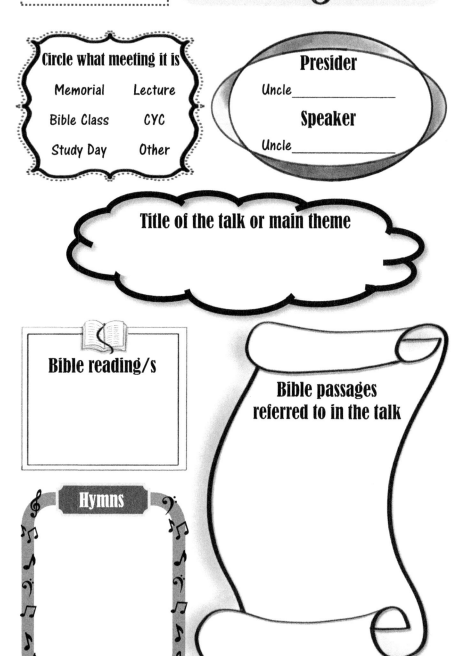

Notes from the talk

_____
_____
_____
_____
_____
_____
_____
_____
_____
_____
_____
_____
_____
_____
_____

Drawing or key verse

Date

Meeting Notes

Circle what meeting it is

Memorial   Lecture

Bible Class   CYC

Study Day   Other

Presider

Uncle_____

Speaker

Uncle_____

Title of the talk or main theme

Bible reading/s

Bible passages referred to in the talk

Hymns

Notes from the talk

_____

_____

_____

_____

_____

_____

_____

_____

_____

_____

_____

_____

_____

_____

_____

Drawing or key verse

Date

Meeting Notes

Circle what meeting it is

Memorial	Lecture
Bible Class	CYC
Study Day	Other

Presider

Uncle_____

Speaker

Uncle_____

Title of the talk or main theme

Bible reading/s

Bible passages referred to in the talk

Hymns

Notes from the talk

_____
_____
_____
_____
_____
_____
_____
_____
_____
_____
_____
_____
_____
_____
_____

Drawing or key verse

Notes from the talk

_____

_____

_____

_____

_____

_____

_____

_____

_____

_____

_____

_____

_____

_____

_____

_____

Drawing or key verse

_____

_____

_____

_____

Date

Meeting Notes

Circle what meeting it is

Memorial   Lecture

Bible Class   CYC

Study Day   Other

Presider

Uncle_____

Speaker

Uncle_____

Title of the talk or main theme

Bible reading/s

Bible passages referred to in the talk

Hymns

Notes from the talk

_____
_____
_____
_____
_____
_____
_____
_____
_____
_____
_____
_____
_____
_____
_____
_____
_____
_____

Drawing or key verse

Date

Meeting Notes

Circle what meeting it is

Memorial	Lecture
Bible Class	CYC
Study Day	Other

Presider

Uncle_____

Speaker

Uncle_____

Title of the talk or main theme

Bible reading/s

Bible passages referred to in the talk

Hymns

Notes from the talk

Drawing or key verse

Date

Meeting Notes

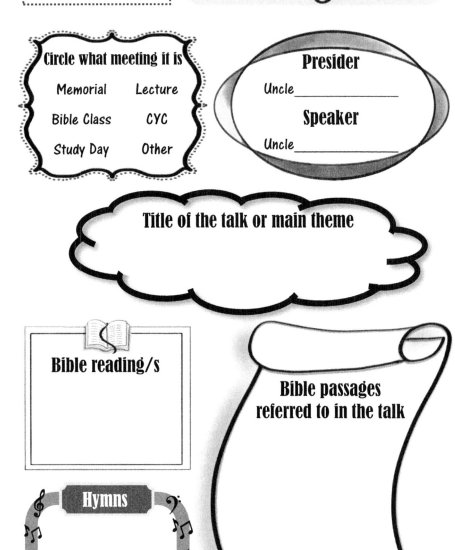

Circle what meeting it is

Memorial   Lecture

Bible Class   CYC

Study Day   Other

Presider

Uncle_____

Speaker

Uncle_____

Title of the talk or main theme

Bible reading/s

Bible passages referred to in the talk

Hymns

Notes from the talk

_____

_____

_____

_____

_____

_____

_____

_____

_____

_____

_____

_____

Drawing or key verse

_____

_____

_____

_____

Notes from the talk

_____
_____
_____
_____
_____
_____
_____
_____
_____
_____
_____
_____
_____
_____
_____

Drawing or key verse

_____
_____
_____
_____

Date

Meeting Notes

Circle what meeting it is

Memorial	Lecture
Bible Class	CYC
Study Day	Other

Presider

Uncle_____

Speaker

Uncle_____

Title of the talk or main theme

Bible reading/s

Bible passages referred to in the talk

Hymns

Notes from the talk

_____

_____

_____

_____

_____

_____

_____

_____

_____

_____

_____

_____

_____

_____

Drawing or key verse

_____

_____

_____

_____

Date

Meeting Notes

Circle what meeting it is

Memorial   Lecture

Bible Class   CYC

Study Day   Other

Presider

Uncle_____

Speaker

Uncle_____

Title of the talk or main theme

Bible reading/s

Bible passages referred to in the talk

Hymns

Notes from the talk

_____

_____

_____

_____

_____

_____

_____

_____

_____

_____

_____

_____

_____

_____

Drawing or key verse

_____

_____

_____

_____

Meeting Notes

Circle what meeting it is

Memorial   Lecture

Bible Class   CYC

Study Day   Other

Presider

Uncle_____

Speaker

Uncle_____

Title of the talk or main theme

Bible reading/s

Bible passages referred to in the talk

Hymns

Notes from the talk

_____

_____

_____

_____

_____

_____

_____

_____

_____

_____

_____

_____

_____

_____

_____

_____

_____

_____

_____

Drawing or key verse

Date

Meeting Notes

Circle what meeting it is

Memorial	Lecture
Bible Class	CYC
Study Day	Other

Presider

Uncle_____

Speaker

Uncle_____

Title of the talk or main theme

Bible reading/s

Bible passages referred to in the talk

Hymns

Notes from the talk

_____

_____

_____

_____

_____

_____

_____

_____

_____

_____

_____

_____

_____

_____

_____

_____

Drawing or key verse

_____

_____

_____

Date

Meeting Notes

Circle what meeting it is

Memorial   Lecture

Bible Class   CYC

Study Day   Other

Presider

Uncle_____

Speaker

Uncle_____

Title of the talk or main theme

Bible reading/s

Bible passages referred to in the talk

Hymns

Notes from the talk

_____

_____

_____

_____

_____

_____

_____

_____

_____

_____

_____

_____

_____

_____

Drawing or key verse

_____

_____

_____

_____

Date

Meeting Notes

Circle what meeting it is

Memorial	Lecture
Bible Class	CYC
Study Day	Other

Presider

Uncle_____

Speaker

Uncle_____

Title of the talk or main theme

Bible reading/s

Bible passages referred to in the talk

Hymns

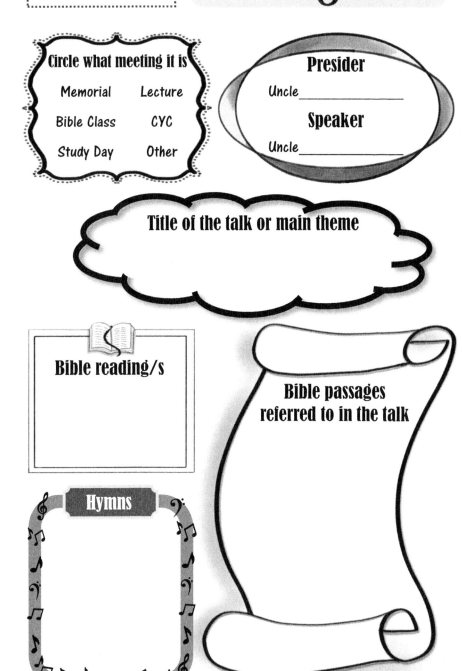

Notes from the talk

_____

_____

_____

_____

_____

_____

_____

_____

_____

_____

_____

_____

_____

Drawing or key verse

_____

_____

_____

Date

Meeting Notes

Circle what meeting it is

Memorial   Lecture

Bible Class   CYC

Study Day   Other

Presider

Uncle_____

Speaker

Uncle_____

Title of the talk or main theme

Bible reading/s

Bible passages referred to in the talk

Hymns

Notes from the talk

_____

_____

_____

_____

_____

_____

_____

_____

_____

_____

_____

_____

_____

_____

_____

Drawing or key verse

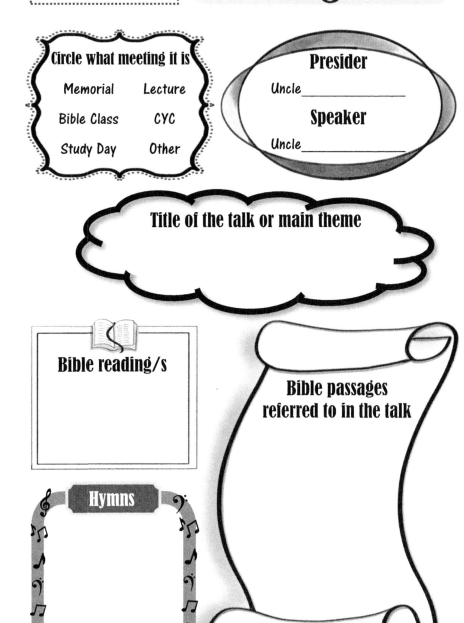

Notes from the talk

_____

_____

_____

_____

_____

_____

_____

_____

_____

_____

_____

_____

_____

_____

_____

Drawing or key verse

Date

Meeting Notes

Circle what meeting it is

Memorial   Lecture

Bible Class   CYC

Study Day   Other

Presider

Uncle_____

Speaker

Uncle_____

Title of the talk or main theme

Bible reading/s

Bible passages referred to in the talk

Hymns

Notes from the talk

_____

_____

_____

_____

_____

_____

_____

_____

_____

_____

_____

_____

_____

_____

_____

_____

_____

Drawing or key verse

Date

Meeting Notes

Circle what meeting it is

Memorial	Lecture
Bible Class	CYC
Study Day	Other

Presider

Uncle_____

Speaker

Uncle_____

Title of the talk or main theme

Bible reading/s

Bible passages referred to in the talk

Hymns

Notes from the talk

_____
_____
_____
_____
_____
_____
_____
_____
_____
_____
_____
_____
_____
_____
_____
_____
_____
_____
_____

Drawing or key verse

Notes from the talk

Drawing or key verse

Date

Meeting Notes

Circle what meeting it is

Memorial	Lecture
Bible Class	CYC
Study Day	Other

Presider

Uncle_____

Speaker

Uncle_____

Title of the talk or main theme

Bible reading/s

Bible passages referred to in the talk

Hymns

Notes from the talk

_____

_____

_____

_____

_____

_____

_____

_____

_____

_____

_____

_____

_____

_____

_____

_____

Drawing or key verse

_____

_____

_____

_____

Meeting Notes

Date

Circle what meeting it is

Memorial	Lecture
Bible Class	CYC
Study Day	Other

Presider

Uncle_____

Speaker

Uncle_____

Title of the talk or main theme

Bible reading/s

Bible passages referred to in the talk

Hymns

Notes from the talk

_____

_____

_____

_____

_____

_____

_____

_____

_____

_____

_____

_____

_____

Drawing or key verse

_____

_____

_____

Date

Meeting Notes

Circle what meeting it is

Memorial	Lecture
Bible Class	CYC
Study Day	Other

Presider

Uncle_____

Speaker

Uncle_____

Title of the talk or main theme

Bible reading/s

Bible passages referred to in the talk

Hymns

Notes from the talk

_____

_____

_____

_____

_____

_____

_____

_____

_____

_____

_____

_____

_____

Drawing or key verse

_____

_____

_____

_____

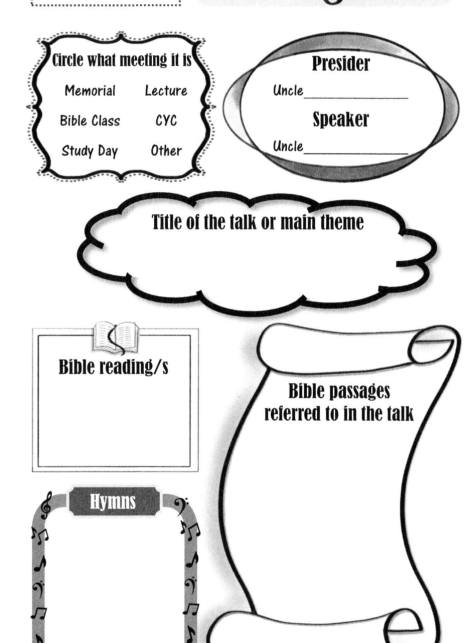

Date

Meeting Notes

Circle what meeting it is

Memorial   Lecture

Bible Class   CYC

Study Day   Other

Presider

Uncle_____

Speaker

Uncle_____

Title of the talk or main theme

Bible reading/s

Bible passages referred to in the talk

Hymns

Notes from the talk

_____

_____

_____

_____

_____

_____

_____

_____

_____

_____

_____

_____

_____

_____

_____

_____

_____

_____

_____

_____

Drawing or key verse

Date

Meeting Notes

Circle what meeting it is

Memorial	Lecture
Bible Class	CYC
Study Day	Other

Presider

Uncle_____

Speaker

Uncle_____

Title of the talk or main theme

Bible reading/s

Bible passages referred to in the talk

Hymns

Notes from the talk

_____

_____

_____

_____

_____

_____

_____

_____

_____

_____

_____

_____

_____

Drawing or key verse

_____

_____

_____

_____

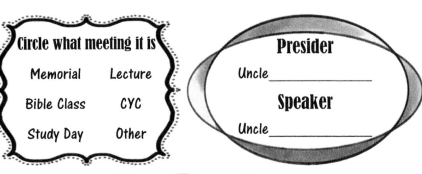

Circle what meeting it is

Memorial   Lecture

Bible Class   CYC

Study Day   Other

Presider

Uncle_____

Speaker

Uncle_____

Title of the talk or main theme

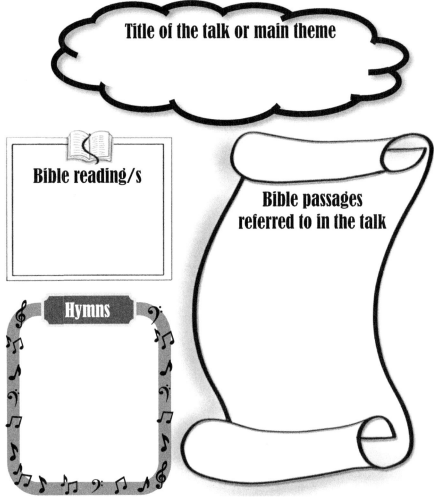

Bible reading/s

Bible passages referred to in the talk

Hymns

Notes from the talk

_____

_____

_____

_____

_____

_____

_____

_____

_____

_____

_____

_____

_____

_____

Drawing or key verse

_____

_____

_____

_____

Date

Meeting Notes

Circle what meeting it is

Memorial	Lecture
Bible Class	CYC
Study Day	Other

Presider

Uncle_____

Speaker

Uncle_____

Title of the talk or main theme

Bible reading/s

Bible passages referred to in the talk

Hymns

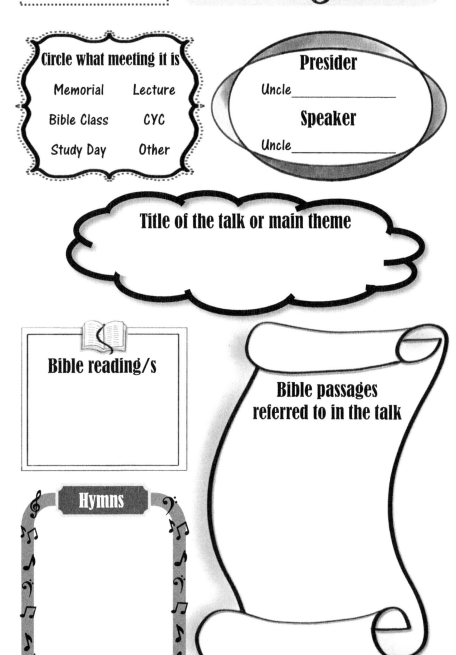

Notes from the talk

_____
_____
_____
_____
_____
_____
_____
_____
_____
_____
_____
_____
_____
_____
_____
_____
_____
_____
_____

Drawing or key verse

Date

Meeting Notes

Circle what meeting it is

Memorial   Lecture

Bible Class   CYC

Study Day   Other

Presider

Uncle_____

Speaker

Uncle_____

Title of the talk or main theme

Bible reading/s

Bible passages referred to in the talk

Hymns

Notes from the talk

_____

_____

_____

_____

_____

_____

_____

_____

_____

_____

_____

_____

_____

_____

_____

_____

Drawing or key verse

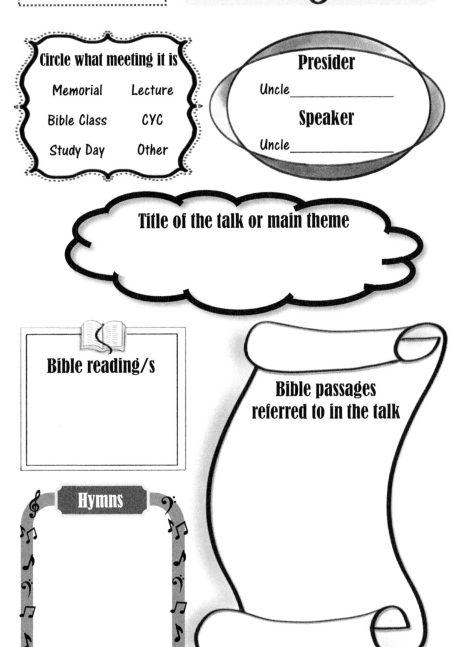

Notes from the talk

_____

_____

_____

_____

_____

_____

_____

_____

_____

_____

_____

_____

_____

Drawing or key verse

Date

Meeting Notes

Circle what meeting it is

Memorial	Lecture
Bible Class	CYC
Study Day	Other

Presider

Uncle_____

Speaker

Uncle_____

Title of the talk or main theme

Bible reading/s

Bible passages referred to in the talk

Hymns

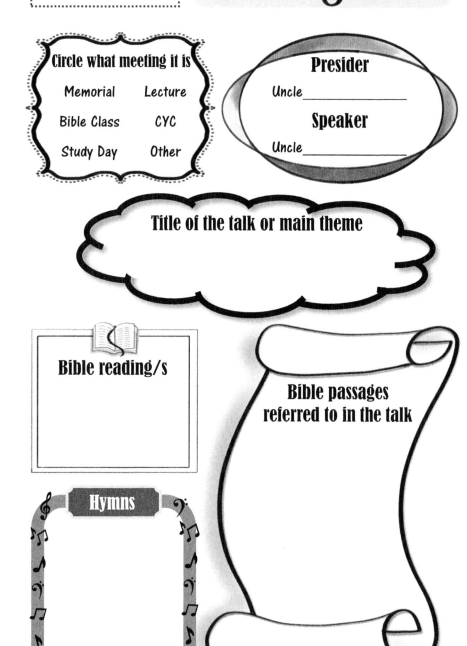

Notes from the talk

_____

_____

_____

_____

_____

_____

_____

_____

_____

_____

_____

_____

_____

_____

_____

Drawing or key verse

_____

_____

_____

_____

Date

Meeting Notes

Circle what meeting it is

Memorial   Lecture

Bible Class   CYC

Study Day   Other

Presider

Uncle _____

Speaker

Uncle _____

Title of the talk or main theme

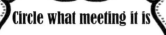

Bible reading/s

Bible passages referred to in the talk

Hymns

Notes from the talk

_____

_____

_____

_____

_____

_____

_____

_____

_____

_____

_____

_____

_____

_____

Drawing or key verse

Date

Meeting Notes

Circle what meeting it is

Memorial   Lecture

Bible Class   CYC

Study Day   Other

Presider

Uncle_____

Speaker

Uncle_____

Title of the talk or main theme

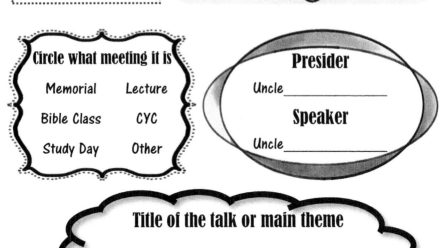

Bible reading/s

Bible passages referred to in the talk

Hymns

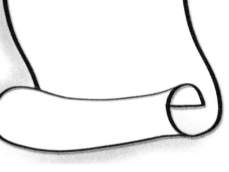

Notes from the talk

_____

_____

_____

_____

_____

_____

_____

_____

_____

_____

_____

_____

_____

_____

_____

Drawing or key verse

Date

Meeting Notes

Circle what meeting it is

Memorial	Lecture
Bible Class	CYC
Study Day	Other

Presider

Uncle_____

Speaker

Uncle_____

Title of the talk or main theme

Bible reading/s

Bible passages referred to in the talk

Hymns

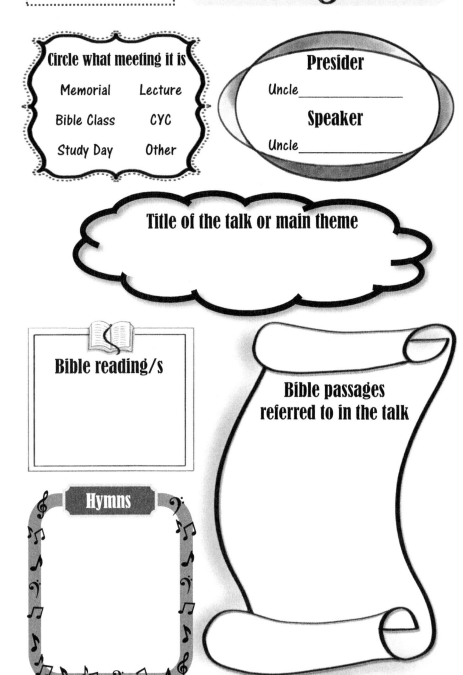

Notes from the talk

_____

_____

_____

_____

_____

_____

_____

_____

_____

_____

_____

_____

_____

_____

_____

_____

Drawing or key verse

_____

_____

_____

_____

_____

Meeting Notes

Circle what meeting it is

Memorial   Lecture

Bible Class   CYC

Study Day   Other

Presider

Uncle_____

Speaker

Uncle_____

Title of the talk or main theme

Bible reading/s

Bible passages referred to in the talk

Hymns

Notes from the talk

_____

_____

_____

_____

_____

_____

_____

_____

_____

_____

_____

_____

_____

_____

_____

_____

_____

Drawing or key verse

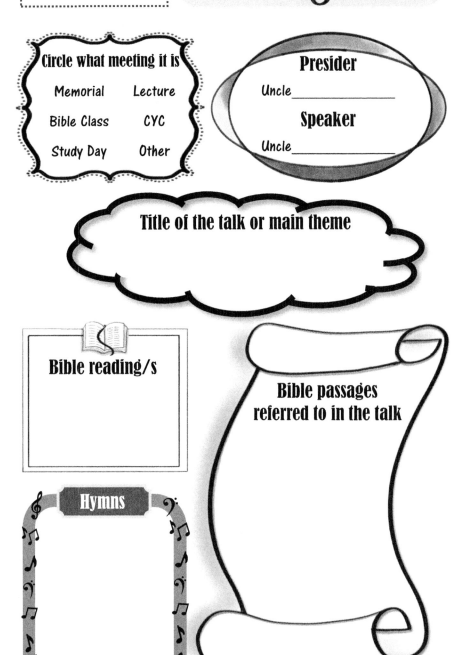

Date

Meeting Notes

Circle what meeting it is

Memorial   Lecture

Bible Class   CYC

Study Day   Other

Presider

Uncle_____

Speaker

Uncle_____

Title of the talk or main theme

Bible reading/s

Bible passages referred to in the talk

Hymns

Notes from the talk

_____

_____

_____

_____

_____

_____

_____

_____

_____

_____

_____

_____

_____

_____

_____

_____

_____

Drawing or key verse

Date

Meeting Notes

Circle what meeting it is

Memorial   Lecture

Bible Class   CYC

Study Day   Other

Presider

Uncle_____

Speaker

Uncle_____

Title of the talk or main theme

Bible reading/s

Bible passages referred to in the talk

Hymns

Notes from the talk

_____

_____

_____

_____

_____

_____

_____

_____

_____

_____

_____

_____

_____

_____

_____

_____

Drawing or key verse

Date

Meeting Notes

Circle what meeting it is

Memorial	Lecture
Bible Class	CYC
Study Day	Other

Presider

Uncle_____

Speaker

Uncle_____

Title of the talk or main theme

Bible reading/s

Bible passages referred to in the talk

Hymns

Notes from the talk

Drawing or key verse

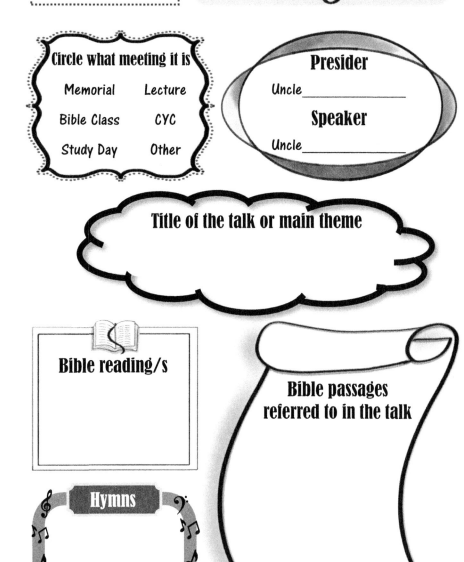

Date

Meeting Notes

Circle what meeting it is

Memorial   Lecture

Bible Class   CYC

Study Day   Other

Presider

Uncle_____

Speaker

Uncle_____

Title of the talk or main theme

Bible reading/s

Bible passages referred to in the talk

Hymns

Notes from the talk

Drawing or key verse

Date

Meeting Notes

Circle what meeting it is

Memorial	Lecture
Bible Class	CYC
Study Day	Other

Presider

Uncle_____

Speaker

Uncle_____

Title of the talk or main theme

Bible reading/s

Bible passages referred to in the talk

Hymns

Notes from the talk

_____
_____
_____
_____
_____
_____
_____
_____
_____
_____
_____
_____
_____
_____
_____
_____
_____

Drawing or key verse

Meeting Notes

Circle what meeting it is

Memorial   Lecture

Bible Class   CYC

Study Day   Other

Presider

Uncle_____

Speaker

Uncle_____

Title of the talk or main theme

Bible reading/s

Bible passages referred to in the talk

Hymns

Notes from the talk

_____

_____

_____

_____

_____

_____

_____

_____

_____

_____

_____

_____

_____

_____

_____

Drawing or key verse

_____

_____

_____

_____

Date

Meeting Notes

Circle what meeting it is

Memorial	Lecture
Bible Class	CYC
Study Day	Other

Presider

Uncle_____

Speaker

Uncle_____

Title of the talk or main theme

Bible reading/s

Bible passages referred to in the talk

Hymns

Notes from the talk

_____

_____

_____

_____

_____

_____

_____

_____

_____

_____

_____

_____

_____

Drawing or key verse

_____

_____

_____

_____

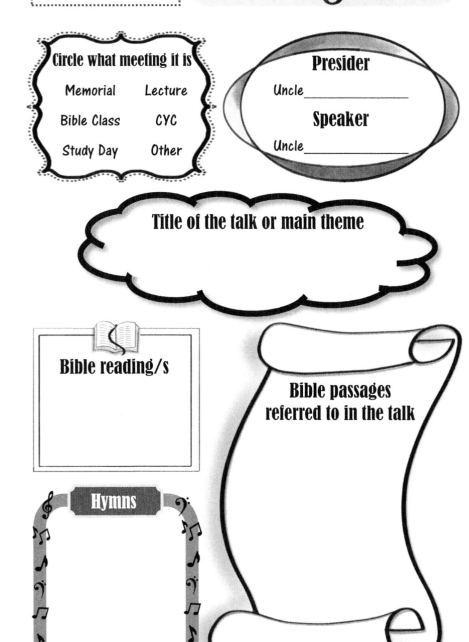

Notes from the talk

_____

_____

_____

_____

_____

_____

_____

_____

_____

_____

_____

_____

_____

_____

_____

_____

_____

Drawing or key verse

_____

_____

_____

_____

Date

Meeting Notes

Circle what meeting it is

Memorial   Lecture

Bible Class   CYC

Study Day   Other

Presider

Uncle_____

Speaker

Uncle_____

Title of the talk or main theme

Bible reading/s

Bible passages referred to in the talk

 **Hymns**

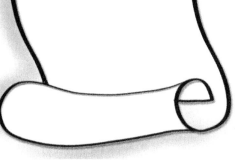

Notes from the talk

_____

_____

_____

_____

_____

_____

_____

_____

_____

_____

_____

_____

_____

_____

_____

_____

_____

_____

Drawing or key verse

Meeting Notes

Circle what meeting it is

Memorial	Lecture
Bible Class	CYC
Study Day	Other

Presider

Uncle_____

Speaker

Uncle_____

Title of the talk or main theme

Bible reading/s

Bible passages referred to in the talk

Hymns

Notes from the talk

_____

_____

_____

_____

_____

_____

_____

_____

_____

_____

_____

_____

_____

_____

Drawing or key verse

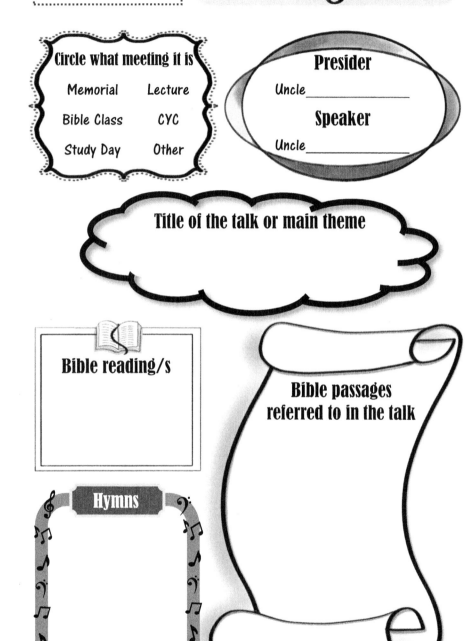

Notes from the talk

Drawing or key verse

Study to shew thyself approved unto God, a workman that needeth not to be ashamed, rightly dividing the word of truth.

2 Timothy 2:15

Printed in Great Britain
by Amazon